VIVALDI

CONCERTO
in A minor, Opus III, No. 6, RV 356

FOR VIOLIN AND PIANO

Published in 2019 by Allegro Editions

Concerto in A minor for Violin and Piano
ISBN: 978-1-9748-9949-4 (paperback)

Cover design by Kaitlyn Whitaker

Cover image: "Violin Front View Isolated on White" by AGCuesta, courtesy of Shutterstock;
"Black and White Piano Keys" by Nerthuz, courtesy of iStock;
"Music Sheet" by danielo, courtesy of Shutterstock

ALLEGRO EDITIONS

CONCERTO
in A minor, Opus III, No. 6, RV 356
for Violin and Piano

Piano reduction from the original by GIUSEPPE PICCIOLI
Violin part edited by IVAN GALAMIAN

ANTONIO VIVALDI
(1678–1741)

Orchestral material available on rental

4

10

CONCERTO
in A minor, for Violin and Piano

PART FOR VIOLIN

CONCERTO
in A minor, Opus III, No. 6, RV 356
for Violin and Piano

VIOLIN

Edited by IVAN GALAMIAN

ANTONIO VIVALDI
(1678–1741)

Orchestral material available on rental